My Favorite Dogs

MINIATURE SCHNAUZER

Jinny Johnson

A⁺
Smart Apple Media

Published by Smart Apple Media,
an imprint of Black Rabbit Books
P.O. Box 3263, Mankato, Minnesota, 56002
www.blackrabbitbooks.com

Edited by Mary-Jane Wilkins
Designed by Hel James

Cataloging-in-Publication Data is available from the Library of Congress

ISBN 978-1-62588-177-9

Photo acknowledgements
title page catolla; 3 Eric Isselee; 4 MaraZe; 5 dezi;
7 Bailey0ne; 8-9, 10 Eric Isselee; 11 Sergey Lavrentev;
11 Eric Isselee/all Shutterstock; 13 adogslifephoto/
Thinkstock; 14 Nikolai Tsvetkov; 15t and b MaraZe;
16 Vladitto; 17 Allison Herreid; 18 Gina Callaway;
19 Raywoo; 20 Sergey Lavrentev; 21 paul geilfuss;
23 littleny
Cover Eric Isselee/Shutterstock

Printed in China

DAD0053
032014
9 8 7 6 5 4 3 2 1

Contents

I'm a Miniature Schnauzer!

I'm small, but I have a big personality and I'm lots of fun.

I'm very active and I love to play. I'll always be your loyal, loving companion, too.

What I Need

I'm happy in the city or the country, as long as I have plenty of exercise every day. I'm not a lap dog and I like to be busy.

Most of all I love company. Please let me be with you as much as possible and don't leave me alone for long.

6

The Miniature Schnauzer

Upright tail
(sometimes docked)

Square, stocky body

Color:
Black, black and silver,
salt and pepper (gray),
white (not recognized
by some breed
associations)

Height:
12-14 inches
(30-36 cm)

Ears high on the head, sometimes cropped to a point

Strong head

Black nose

Bushy beard, mustache, and eyebrows

Rough, wiry coat

9

All About Miniature Schnauzers

Schnauzers come from Germany and may have been around since the 1400s. Miniatures were probably bred from Standard Schnauzers, Affenpinschers, and poodles.

The first Miniature Schnauzers were farm dogs, used to catch rats.

Now they are bred as companions, but they are still sturdy, energetic little dogs.

Schnauzers

There are two other Schnauzer breeds.

The Standard is a medium-sized dog that stands about 19 inches (48 cm) high. This German breed was used as a guard dog and for catching rats.

The Giant
Schnauzer can
be 27.5 inches
(70 cm) tall.
It is a powerful
animal with the
same square head
and body shape
as the Miniature.

It makes a good
guard dog and
a loyal friend.

Growing Up

A Miniature Schnauzer, like all pups, needs to be with her mom and brothers and sisters until she is eight weeks old. Then she will be ready to join her new family.

Everything may seem strange to her at first and a little scary.

Be extra
gentle with
your new
pup and
help her
settle in.
She will
soon feel
part of her
new family.

Training Your Dog

Miniature Schnauzers are smart, obedient, and learn quickly, so they are easy to train. Make sure your dog knows who is boss right from the start, so she will behave well.

Well-trained Schnauzers are good with children

and make great companions for older people.

The Miniature Schnauzer's bouncy, energetic nature helps her shine at agility trials.

Schnauzers are good guard dogs, too. They will always let you know if a stranger comes to the door.

Watch Out!

Miniature Schnauzers are alert, lively little dogs. They love to run. Watch out, though—a Schnauzer can't resist chasing a rat or mouse and will race off after them.

Be careful if you have small pets such as hamsters. A Schnauzer will want to chase them, too.

Teach your
dog that small
pets are out
of bounds
and
never
leave
the
animals
alone
together.

Your Healthy Dog

Schnauzers have a double coat–
a soft undercoat and a rough, wiry
topcoat. It is easy to care for, but
should be brushed and combed
regularly. The
coat will also
need clipping
twice a year.

Schnauzers gain
weight easily,

so don't give them too many treats.

This breed is ideal for anyone with an allergy to dog hair, as it does not shed much hair.

Miniature Schnauzers can suffer from eye problems and other diseases. Be sure to buy your puppy from a good breeder.

Caring for Your Dog

You and your family must think very carefully before buying a Miniature Schnauzer. She may live for 15 years.

Every day your dog must have food, water, and exercise, and lots of love and care. She will need to go to the vet regularly. When your family goes out or away, you must plan for your dog to be looked after.

Useful Words

agility trials
Events where dogs run around
courses with obstacles and jumps.

breed
A particular type of dog.

vaccination
An injection that can help to
protect your dog from illness.

Index